D1710061

SandCastle™
Baby Animals

Bunnies

Alex Kuskowski

A Division of ABDO

ABDO
Publishing Company

Consulting Editor, Diane Craig, M.A./Reading Specialist

visit us at www.abdopublishing.com

Published by ABDO Publishing Company, a division of ABDO, P.O. Box 398166, Minneapolis, Minnesota 55439. Copyright © 2014 by Abdo Consulting Group, Inc. International copyrights reserved in all countries. No part of this book may be reproduced in any form without written permission from the publisher. SandCastle™ is a trademark and logo of ABDO Publishing Company.

Printed in the United States of America, North Mankato, Minnesota
062013
012014

 PRINTED ON RECYCLED PAPER

Editor: Liz Salzmann
Content Developer: Alex Kuskowski
Cover and Interior Design and Production: Mighty Media, Inc.
Photo Credits: Shutterstock, Thinkstock

Library of Congress Cataloging-in-Publication Data

Kuskowski, Alex.
  Bunnies / by Alex Kuskowski ; consulting editor, Diane Craig, M.A., reading specialist.
     pages cm. -- (Baby animals)
  Audience: Ages 4-9.
  ISBN 978-1-61783-835-4
1. Rabbits--Infancy--Juvenile literature. I. Title.
  QL737.L32K87 2014
  599.3213'92--dc23
                          2012049660

SandCastle™ Level: Beginning

SandCastle™ books are created by a team of professional educators, reading specialists, and content developers around five essential components—phonemic awareness, phonics, vocabulary, text comprehension, and fluency—to assist young readers as they develop reading skills and strategies and increase their general knowledge. All books are written, reviewed, and leveled for guided reading, early reading intervention, and Accelerated Reader® programs for use in shared, guided, and independent reading and writing activities to support a balanced approach to literacy instruction. The SandCastle™ series has four levels that correspond to early literacy development. The levels are provided to help teachers and parents select appropriate books for young readers.

| Emerging Readers (no flags) | Beginning Readers (1 flag) | Transitional Readers (2 flags) | Fluent Readers (3 flags) |

Contents

Bunnies

A baby rabbit is called a bunny. Some bunnies live in the wild. Some bunnies are pets.

Bunnies have brothers and sisters. Bunnies born together are called a **litter** of bunnies.

Juan's bunny **nibbles** on a carrot. Bunnies eat grass and hay too.

Flopsy has long ears.
Bunnies can hear sounds
from a long way away.

Wild bunnies sleep during the day. They come out to eat at **dawn** and **dusk**.

Maya has a lot of pet bunnies. **Male** bunnies are called bucks. **Female** bunnies are called does.

Bunnies have fur.
It keeps them warm and
dry. They lick their fur to
stay clean.

Blake plays with his bunny Mopsy. Bunnies are calm and quiet pets.

Bunnies can be trained.
Anna teaches her bunny
to jump over a fence.

Did You Know?

▶ A bunny's eyes are on the side of its head. It can see every direction without turning around.

▶ The only kind of wild bunny that doesn't live in a **burrow** is the cottontail.

▶ Six months after being born, a bunny is a full-grown rabbit.

▶ Bunnies have four toes on each back foot. They have five toes on each front foot.

Bunny Quiz

Read each sentence below. Then decide whether it is true or false.

1. Bunnies never have brothers or sisters.

2. Bunnies can hear sounds from a long way away.

3. Bunnies always come out to eat in the middle of the day.

4. **Male** bunnies are called bucks.

5. Bunnies are loud pets.

Answers: 1. False 2. True 3. False 4. True 5. False

Glossary

· ·

burrow – a hole or tunnel dug in the ground by a small animal for use as shelter.

dawn – the time of day when the sky grows lighter and the sun rises.

dusk – the time of day when the sky grows darker and the sun sets.

female – being of the sex that can produce eggs or give birth. Mothers are female.

litter – a group of baby animals, such as bunnies, born at the same time.

male – being of the sex that can father offspring. Fathers are male.

nibble – to eat using small bites.